From the Valley to the Summit: A Journey of Resilience and Impact

From the Valley to the Summit: A Journey of Resilience and Impact
Written by DeShaun Williams

Copyright © 2024 by DeShaun Williams Industries, LLC

All rights reserved. No part of this book may be reproduced, distributed, or transmitted in any form or by any means, including photocopying, recording, or other electronic or mechanical methods, without the prior written permission of the publisher, except in the case of brief quotations embodied in critical reviews and certain other noncommercial uses permitted by copyright law.

To my grandparents,
whose unwavering love and support
taught me the true meaning of resilience
and strength.

To all those who have faced valleys of hardship,
may you find the courage to climb to
your own summits.

And to everyone who believes in the
power of positive change,
this book is for you.

Table of Contents

Chapter 1...........................The Ascent Begins

Chapter 2................ Trust in the Inner Circle

Chapter 3.......... Reaching the Mountaintop

Chapter 4............................ The Betrayal

Chapter 5............................ The Fall

Chapter 6...................... Rebuilding the Climb

Chapter 7................... A New Vision

Chapter 8...................... Finding Balance

Chapter 9................... Embracing Change

Chapter 10................ Legacy of Impact

Chapter 11... Reflections and New Horizons

Chapter 1: The Ascent Begins

The early morning sun peeked over the horizon, casting a warm glow on the small town nestled in the valley. For many, it was just another day, but for James, it was the beginning of something greater. Standing at the foot of the towering mountain that loomed over his hometown, he felt a sense of purpose and determination that he had not felt in years.

James had always been a dreamer. From an early age, he imagined himself conquering great heights, not just physically, but metaphorically. Growing up in a modest household, he was no stranger to hard work and perseverance. His parents, though loving, struggled to make ends meet, and James often found himself taking on responsibilities beyond his years. But it was these early challenges that shaped his character, instilling in him a relentless drive to succeed.

As a teenager, James discovered his passion for climbing. It started with a trip to a nearby rock wall with friends, where he quickly realized he had a natural talent for the sport. The thrill of scaling heights, the adrenaline rush, and the sense of accomplishment that came with reaching the top fueled his ambition. Climbing became his escape, his way of pushing beyond the limitations of his circumstances.

James's journey to the mountaintop wasn't just about physical climbing; it was about rising above the obstacles life threw at him. He excelled in school, balancing his studies with part-time jobs to help support his family. His dedication caught the attention of teachers and mentors who saw potential in him and encouraged him to pursue higher education. With their guidance, James earned a scholarship to a prestigious university, marking the first major milestone in his ascent.

University life was a whirlwind of new experiences and opportunities. James immersed himself in his studies, majoring in engineering, a field that fascinated him with its blend of problem-solving and innovation. He joined the university's climbing club, quickly establishing himself as a standout member. His peers admired his skill and determination, and he formed bonds with fellow climbers who shared his passion.

However, the journey was not without its struggles. Balancing academics, work, and climbing was a constant challenge. There were moments of doubt and exhaustion, times when he questioned whether he could continue pushing forward. But every time he wanted to give up, he remembered the look of pride in his parents' eyes when he left for university, and it reignited his resolve.

James's ascent was marked by a series of triumphs that further fueled his ambition. He competed in regional climbing competitions, often finishing at the top. His academic achievements garnered him internships with renowned engineering firms, providing invaluable experience and networking opportunities. Yet, through it all, he remained humble, never forgetting the support and encouragement that had brought him this far.

As graduation approached, James stood at the precipice of a new chapter in his life. Armed with a degree and a wealth of experiences, he was ready to tackle the professional world. He secured a position at a leading engineering company, a dream job that promised growth and advancement. It felt like he had finally reached the summit he had been striving for all these years.

But standing on the mountaintop, James could not shake the feeling that there was more to his journey. He had achieved so much, yet he knew that true success was not just about personal accomplishments. It was about making a difference, lifting others as he climbed. Little did he know that this realization would soon be put to the test, as the challenges he would face next would push him to his limits and beyond.

In this moment of triumph, James felt a sense of contentment, but also a stirring of anticipation. The mountain had taught him that every ascent is followed by a descent, and it is in those valleys that true character is forged. As he looked out over the horizon, he could not have imagined the trials that awaited him, nor the profound lessons they would impart. For now, he embraced the journey, ready to face whatever came next with the same resilience and determination that had brought him this far.

Chapter 2: Trust in the Inner Circle

With his degree in hand and a promising job at a leading engineering firm, James felt like he was finally stepping into the life he had always envisioned. The corporate world was a new kind of mountain to climb, full of its own unique challenges and opportunities. It was here that James began to build a network of colleagues and friends, creating an inner circle of trust that would become crucial to his journey.

From the outset, James was determined to make a strong impression. He worked long hours, took on complex projects, and consistently delivered results that exceeded expectations. His dedication did not go unnoticed. Senior executives began to see him as a rising star within the company, and his peers admired his work ethic and drive. Among them, he found a few individuals who would become his closest friends and confidants.

There was Sarah, a brilliant software engineer with a sharp mind and a kind heart. They had met during orientation, bonding over their shared love of climbing and a mutual respect for each other's talents. Sarah became James's sounding board, the person he turned to for advice and support both professionally and personally.

Then there was Michael, a charismatic project manager with a knack for bringing people together. Michael had an infectious energy and a way of making everyone feel included. He quickly became a central figure in their social circle, organizing outings and team-building activities that strengthened their bonds.

Lastly, there was Rachel, a finance expert with a pragmatic approach to problem-solving. Rachel's no-nonsense attitude and unwavering loyalty made her someone James could rely on when things got tough. She was the voice of reason, the one who kept the group grounded and focused on their goals.

Together, they formed a tight-knit group, sharing not just professional ambitions but personal dreams and struggles as well. They celebrated each other's successes and provided comfort during setbacks. It was a camaraderie built on mutual respect, trust, and a shared commitment to helping each other succeed.

As the months turned into years, their friendships deepened. They navigated the corporate ladder together, facing the pressures and politics of the business world with a united front. James thrived in this environment, drawing strength from his inner circle. He quickly rose through the ranks, earning promotions and taking on leadership roles that showcased his skills and vision.

Outside of work, their bond grew stronger. They spent weekends hiking and climbing, adventures that reminded James of the importance of balance and connection. These moments of escape, away from the pressures of their careers, provided a much-needed respite and a chance to reinforce their trust in one another.

But as their professional lives became increasingly intertwined, the lines between friendship and competition began to blur. The corporate world was fiercely competitive, and the stakes were high. While their bond remained strong, subtle tensions started to surface. The pressure to succeed, coupled with the fear of failure, created cracks in the foundation of their relationships.

For James, these were trying times. He was torn between his loyalty to his friends and his drive to excel. He found himself questioning decisions, second-guessing motives, and struggling to maintain the trust that had once seemed unshakeable. The camaraderie that had been a source of strength now felt like a delicate balancing act.

Despite the challenges, James remained optimistic. He believed in the strength of their bond and was determined to navigate these turbulent waters with integrity and transparency. He trusted that, in the end, their friendship would prevail over the pressures of the corporate world.

However, as the pressures mounted, so did the complexity of their relationships. Ambitions clashed, misunderstandings grew, and the unspoken tensions threatened to unravel the fabric of their trust. James found himself at a crossroads, facing a choice that would test the very foundation of his inner circle.

It was during this period of uncertainty that James would come to realize that trust, like any climb, required constant effort and vigilance. The lessons he had learned on the physical mountains would now be applied to the metaphorical ones, as he prepared to face the greatest challenge of his journey: maintaining integrity and resilience in the face of betrayal.

In the heart of these trials, James would discover the true meaning of trust and the strength it took to rebuild it once shattered. Little did he know, this chapter of his life would set the stage for the ultimate test of his character and resolve, forging a path that would lead him back to the mountaintop in ways he never expected.

Chapter 3: Reaching the Mountaintop

James stood at the edge of the cliff, the cool mountain air filling his lungs as he gazed out at the expanse below. It was a familiar view, yet this time it carried a different weight. He had reached the pinnacle of his professional journey, a moment that signified not just personal achievement but the culmination of years of relentless effort, sacrifice, and growth. It was a view he had long dreamed of, but never quite imagined would feel so profound.

The path to this point had been steep and grueling. James had poured his heart and soul into every project, every challenge, and every opportunity that came his way. His innovative ideas and exceptional leadership had propelled him to the position of Senior Vice President at his firm, a role that came with immense responsibility and influence. He was now at the helm of major projects, shaping the future of the company and mentoring the next generation of engineers.

The ascent had not been easy. The corporate world was a battleground of ambition and competition, where only the strongest and most resilient survived. James had faced countless obstacles, from tight deadlines and budget constraints to office politics and power struggles. But through it all, he had remained steadfast, driven by a vision of success that extended beyond personal gain to encompass a broader impact.

One of the projects that marked a turning point in his career was the development of a groundbreaking renewable energy system. It was a complex and ambitious endeavor, one that required not only technical expertise but also the ability to lead and inspire a diverse team of professionals. James's ability to bring people together, to harness their strengths and foster a spirit of collaboration, was instrumental in the project's success.

As the project neared completion, it became clear that they were on the verge of something monumental. The energy system promised to revolutionize the industry, offering sustainable solutions that could significantly reduce the carbon footprint and provide clean energy to millions. The recognition and accolades that followed were a testament to the hard work and dedication of everyone involved, but for James, it was a personal triumph that validated years of perseverance.

The success of the renewable energy project catapulted James into the spotlight. He was invited to speak at conferences, featured in industry publications, and sought after for his insights and expertise. His ascent to the mountaintop was celebrated not just within his company but across the entire industry. It was a moment of pride and fulfillment, a testament to what could be achieved through determination and vision.

Yet, as James stood at the summit, basking in the glow of his achievements, he could not shake the feeling that something was missing. The journey had been exhilarating, but it had also been isolating. The higher he climbed, the more distant he felt from the camaraderie and trust that had once been the bedrock of his success. The friendships that had sustained him through the early years now seemed strained, shadowed by unspoken tensions and unresolved conflicts.

Michael, once the glue that held their group together, had become increasingly distant. His own ambitions had taken him in a different direction, and the easy rapport they once shared was now replaced by a professional rivalry that neither acknowledged but both felt. Sarah, always a source of wisdom and support, seemed preoccupied with her own challenges, and their conversations, once rich and meaningful, had grown stilted and rare. Rachel remained a steadfast ally, but even her pragmatic counsel could not bridge the growing chasm between them.

James found himself reflecting on the cost of his ascent. Success had brought recognition and respect, but it had also exacted a toll on the relationships that mattered most to him. He realized that reaching the mountaintop was not just about personal achievement; it was about the journey and the people who walked it with him. In his pursuit of excellence, he had lost sight of the very things that had given his journey meaning.

Determined to reclaim the bonds that had once been his foundation, James decided to act. He reached out to Sarah, Michael, and Rachel, suggesting a weekend retreat in the mountains where they could reconnect and reflect. It was a bold move, one that required vulnerability and courage, but James knew it was necessary. They needed to address the unspoken tensions, to heal the rifts that had formed, and to rebuild the trust that had been eroded by the pressures of their climb.

The retreat was a turning point. Away from the distractions and demands of their professional lives, they were able to rediscover the friendship and trust that had once been so natural. They shared their fears, their frustrations, and their hopes, finding common ground and renewed purpose. It was a reminder that success was not a solitary endeavor but a collective journey, one that required mutual support and understanding.

As James left the mountains with his friends, he felt a renewed sense of clarity and purpose. The view from the mountaintop was beautiful, but it was the journey, with all its trials and triumphs, that truly defined him. He realized that his greatest achievement was not the position he held or the projects he led, but the enduring strength and resilience of the relationships that had sustained him along the way.

In the chapters that lay ahead, James would face new challenges and opportunities, but he was ready. He had learned that true success was not just about reaching the summit but about maintaining the integrity, inclusiveness, and trust that made the journey worthwhile. And as he prepared to navigate the peaks and valleys that lay before him, he knew he would do so with the strength and support of those who had climbed with him, every step of the way.

Chapter 4: The Betrayal

James's newfound clarity and reconnection with his friends infused him with a renewed sense of purpose as he returned to his work. He felt invigorated, ready to take on new challenges with the support of his inner circle. However, life has a way of testing even the strongest bonds, and it was not long before James faced a trial that would shake his trust to its core.

The first sign of trouble came in the form of a major project proposal. The firm had landed a high-profile contract to design and implement an innovative infrastructure system for a metropolitan city—a project that promised to be a game-changer for both the company and the city itself. James was appointed the lead, a testament to his skills and leadership. It was an opportunity of a lifetime, and he eagerly dove into the work, assembling a team that included his closest friends.

As the project progressed, the pressures mounted. Deadlines loomed, budgets tightened, and the stakes grew higher with each passing day. It was during this intense period that James noticed subtle shifts in his relationships with Michael, Sarah, and Rachel. Meetings that had once been collaborative and open now felt strained and guarded. There were whispered conversations, furtive glances, and an underlying tension that James could not quite put his finger on.

One evening, after a particularly grueling day, James decided to confront Michael, hoping to clear the air. They met at a quiet bar near the office, a place where they had shared many candid conversations in the past. James expressed his concerns, trying to understand what was causing the rift between them. Michael's response was evasive, his usual charm replaced by a defensive edge. He spoke of pressures from upper management, of conflicting priorities, but James sensed there was more to it.

Over the next few weeks, the situation escalated. James noticed discrepancies in the project's financial reports and delays that could not be easily explained. When he questioned Sarah and Rachel, they seemed uncomfortable and evasive. It became clear that something was being hidden from him, and his growing unease turned into suspicion.

Determined to find the underlying cause of it, James started digging deeper. He reviewed emails, scrutinized reports, and conducted private meetings with team members. What he uncovered left him reeling. Michael had been diverting funds from the project to finance a side venture, a startup he had secretly been working on. Sarah and Rachel, though not directly involved, had known about it and chose to remain silent, fearing the repercussions of speaking out.

The betrayal cut deep. These were the people he had trusted implicitly, the friends who had stood by him through thick and thin. The realization that they had been complicit in deceiving him was a blow that struck at the very heart of his trust. James felt a profound sense of loss, not just for the project but for the friendships he had cherished.

In the days that followed, James grappled with a whirlwind of emotions—anger, disappointment, and a profound sense of betrayal. He confronted Michael, demanding an explanation. Michael, cornered and defensive, admitted to his actions but tried to justify them as a necessary risk for his future. James's heart sank as he listened to Michael's rationalizations, realizing that their friendship had been sacrificed on the altar of ambition.

Sarah and Rachel's reactions were equally heartbreaking. They expressed regret for their silence but struggled to fully explain why they had not come forward. Their fear of jeopardizing their careers and the potential fallout had outweighed their loyalty to James. It was a harsh lesson in the fragility of trust and the complex dynamics of professional relationships.

The fallout was swift and severe. James reported the misconduct to upper management, and an internal investigation was launched. Michael was terminated, and Sarah and Rachel faced disciplinary actions. The project, now tainted by scandal, faced delays and additional scrutiny. James found himself at the center of a storm, trying to salvage what remained of his professional integrity and the project he had worked so hard to bring to fruition.

The betrayal left a lasting scar on James's heart. It forced him to reevaluate his understanding of trust, loyalty, and the full cost of ambition. He had always believed that success was a collective journey, built on mutual support and integrity. This experience shattered that belief, leaving him questioning not just his friendships but his own judgment.

In the aftermath, James turned inward, seeking solace in reflection and introspection. He leaned on the lessons he had learned from climbing—how to endure, how to navigate the harshest terrains, and how to find strength amid adversity. He realized that while the betrayal had shaken him to his core, it had also revealed an inner resilience he had not fully recognized.

Determined to move forward, James focused on rebuilding. He poured his energy into the project, determined to see it through to completion despite the setbacks. He reached out to new team members, fostering a culture of transparency and accountability. He also sought out therapy and mentorship, recognizing the need for guidance and support in navigating the emotional aftermath of the betrayal.

Through this painful chapter, James emerged with a deeper understanding of himself and the complexities of human relationships. He learned that trust, once broken, could be rebuilt, but it required time, effort, and a willingness to forgive—not just others, but himself. The journey to the mountaintop was not just about reaching the summit but about finding the strength to rise again after every fall.

As James prepared to face the challenges ahead, he carried with him the scars of betrayal but also the wisdom and resilience that came from overcoming it. The path to redemption was long and arduous, but he was ready to walk it, one step at a time, with the unwavering belief that true success was found not in the heights he reached, but in the depth of his character and the strength of his heart.

Chapter 5: The Fall

James sat alone in his office, the dim light from his desk lamp casting long shadows on the walls. The silence was heavy, filled with the weight of recent events. The betrayal by Michael, Sarah, and Rachel had not just shaken his trust—it had shattered it. As he stared at the stack of project documents in front of him, he felt an overwhelming sense of despair.

The internal investigation had concluded, and the firm had made its decisions. Michael was gone, and Sarah and Rachel were demoted and reassigned to different departments. The project, once a beacon of hope and innovation, now stood as a monument to deception and misplaced trust. The delays and budget overruns were significant, and the additional scrutiny from upper management was relentless.

Despite his efforts to salvage the project, James could not shake the feeling that he had failed. He felt responsible for not seeing the signs earlier, for trusting too easily, and for allowing his friendships to cloud his judgment. The confidence and optimism that had fueled his ascent seemed to have evaporated, leaving behind a void filled with self-doubt and regret.

The emotional toll was immense. James found it difficult to sleep, his mind racing with thoughts of what he could have done differently. He withdrew from his colleagues, avoiding the water cooler conversations and after-work gatherings that once brought him joy. The isolation only deepened his sense of loneliness and despair.

Outside of work, the impact was just as profound. James had always found solace in climbing, but now even the mountains felt tainted by the betrayal. He struggled to find the motivation to lace up his boots and hit the trails. The physical and mental exhaustion was too great, and the thought of facing another climb felt insurmountable.

His relationship with his family also suffered. His parents, proud of his achievements and always supportive, were worried about the change in their son. They reached out, offering words of encouragement and love, but James found it hard to open to them. He did not want to burden them with his pain, so he put on a brave face, hiding the turmoil that raged within.

In his darkest moments, James questioned everything. Was the climb worth it? Had he sacrificed too much for success? He wondered if he had lost sight of what truly mattered. The values of integrity, trust, and loyalty that had guided him now felt like distant ideals, overshadowed by the harsh realities of betrayal and ambition.

One evening, after a particularly grueling day at work, James found himself standing on a bridge overlooking the city. The view was breathtaking, but it offered little comfort. The cars below moved like ants, oblivious to his internal struggle. As he leaned against the railing, the weight of his thoughts pressed down on him.

It was then that he remembered a quote from his favorite climbing mentor: "The summit is what drives us, but the climb itself is what matters." Those words had always inspired him, reminding him to find joy and meaning in the journey, not just the destination. But now, standing on the edge, he struggled to see how they applied to his life.

Just as he was about to turn away, his phone buzzed. It was a message from an old friend, someone he had not spoken to in years. The timing was uncanny, as if the universe had sensed his need for connection. The message was simple: "Thinking of you. Let's catch up soon."

That small gesture of kindness was enough to pull James back from the brink. It reminded him that, despite the betrayal and the pain, there were still people who cared about him. He realized that he did not have to face this alone, and that perhaps, reaching out for help was a sign of strength, not weakness.

Determined to find a way forward, James sought out a therapist. He knew that he needed to confront his emotions head-on, to process the betrayal and the impact it had on his life. Therapy was a new and daunting step, but it was also a necessary one. Through the sessions, James began to unpack the layers of hurt and guilt, slowly rebuilding his sense of self.

He also reached out to a mentor from his climbing days, someone who had always provided wisdom and guidance. Their conversations were a lifeline, offering perspective and reminding James of the resilience he had developed over the years. The mentor encouraged him to return to the mountains, not as an escape, but to reconnect with his true self.

With time and support, James began to find his footing again. He started climbing once more, each ascent a reminder of his inner strength and determination. The physical challenge helped him clear his mind, and the beauty of the mountains provided a sense of peace that he had desperately missed.

At work, James adopted an innovative approach. He focused on rebuilding trust within his team, fostering a culture of transparency and accountability. He implemented stricter oversight and encouraged open communication, determined to prevent a repeat of the past. It was a slow process, but gradually, the project began to regain momentum.

James also made amends with Sarah and Rachel. While their actions had hurt him deeply, he recognized that holding onto resentment would only hinder his own healing. Through honest conversations, they acknowledged their mistakes and the pain they had caused. It was not an easy path, but forgiveness offered a way to move forward.

As he stood on a mountain peak one crisp morning, James reflected on the journey that had brought him there. The betrayal and the fall had tested him in ways he had never imagined, but they had also revealed his resilience and capacity for growth. He understood now that the climb was not just about reaching the summit but about navigating the valleys and finding strength in adversity.

James knew that there would be more challenges ahead, but he was ready to face them with renewed purpose and integrity. The fall had been painful, but it had also been a powerful teacher, shaping him into a stronger, more compassionate leader. And as he looked out at the horizon, he felt a deep sense of gratitude for the journey, with all its highs and lows, knowing that it was the climb itself that truly mattered.

Chapter 6: Rebuilding the Climb

James stood in the conference room, a sea of faces looking back at him. It was the first major meeting since the fallout, and the tension was palpable. The project, once tainted by scandal, was now in a critical phase. James had spent the past months working tirelessly to regain control, to rebuild trust, and to steer the team toward success. Today's meeting was a pivotal moment, a chance to set a new tone and direction.

He took a deep breath and began. "We've all been through a lot," he started, his voice steady but filled with emotion. "This project has faced challenges we could not have anticipated. But we are still here, and we have an opportunity to turn this around. To not just complete this project, but to do it with integrity and excellence."

The room was silent, everyone hanging on his words. James continued, outlining a clear plan of action, setting new goals, and emphasizing the importance of teamwork and transparency. He spoke from the heart, acknowledging past mistakes and highlighting the lessons learned. By the end of the meeting, the atmosphere had shifted. There was a sense of cautious optimism, a collective willingness to move forward together.

The months that followed were a test of everything James had learned. The road was far from smooth, with countless obstacles and setbacks. But he was no longer climbing alone. The team rallied around him; each person committed to the vision he had laid out. They worked long hours, navigated bureaucratic hurdles, and solved complex technical issues. Slowly but surely, progress was made.

James found solace in the routine of climbing. Each weekend, he would escape to the mountains, finding peace and clarity in the physical challenge. These climbs became a metaphor for his journey with the project—each step a reminder of the resilience and determination needed to reach the summit.

One crisp autumn morning, James stood at the base of a particularly challenging peak. It was a climb he had attempted once before, years ago, but had never completed. Today, he felt ready. As he ascended, he reflected on the parallels between this climb and his professional journey. There were moments of doubt, stretches where the path was unclear, and times when he had to dig deep to find the strength to continue. But with each step, he moved closer to the summit.

Reaching the top, James was greeted by a breathtaking view. The valley below stretched out in a tapestry of autumn colors, the sky a brilliant blue. He stood there, taking it all in, feeling a profound sense of accomplishment. The climb had been difficult, but it had also been transformative. It reminded him that the journey, with all its challenges, was what truly defined the experience.

Back at the office, the project was nearing completion. The team had managed to overcome the odds, delivering innovative solutions, and meeting critical milestones. The city's new infrastructure system was poised to set a benchmark in sustainability and efficiency. It was a triumph born from adversity, a testament to the power of resilience and teamwork.

On the day of the project's final presentation, James felt a mix of pride and gratitude. He addressed the stakeholders, outlining the journey and the remarkable efforts of the team. The response was overwhelmingly positive, with accolades and recognition pouring in from all sides. The project was hailed as a success, and James's leadership was widely praised.

In the aftermath of the project's completion, James took some time to reflect on his journey. The betrayal, the fall, and the climb back had taught him invaluable lessons about trust, leadership, and the importance of staying true to one's values. He had emerged stronger, more compassionate, and more aware of the complexities of human relationships.

James reached out to Michael, Sarah, and Rachel. While their paths had diverged, he felt it was important to acknowledge the past and find closure. The conversations were difficult but necessary, allowing them all to express their regrets and move forward. Forgiveness, James realized, was not just about absolving others, but also about freeing himself from the weight of resentment.

As he prepared for the next phase of his career, James felt a renewed sense of purpose. He had weathered one of the toughest storms of his life and had come out the other side with a deeper understanding of what it meant to lead with integrity and compassion. He was ready to take on new challenges, knowing that the strength he had gained from his experiences would guide him.

The journey to the mountaintop was ongoing, filled with new peaks and valleys. But James was no longer focused solely on the summit. He had learned to value the climb itself, to find meaning in each step and to appreciate the people who walked the path with him. And as he looked to the horizon, he felt a profound sense of gratitude for the journey, with all its trials and triumphs, knowing that it was the climb that truly mattered.

Chapter 7: A New Vision

James had always been driven by his goals; his eyes fixed firmly on the future. But after the tumultuous journey he had endured, he realized it was time to reassess his path. The completion of the city's infrastructure project had been a significant achievement, yet it felt like the end of one chapter and the beginning of another. He was ready to explore new horizons, both personally and professionally.

One of the first changes James made was to create more balance in his life. He had spent years prioritizing work, often at the expense of his well-being and personal relationships. Now, he made a conscious effort to carve out time for the things that brought him joy. He returned to his love for climbing, not just as an escape but to reconnect with nature and himself. The mountains became his sanctuary, a place where he could reflect, recharge, and find clarity.

James also began volunteering at a local community center, mentoring young people who were interested in engineering and technology. He saw himself in these eager, bright-eyed individuals, and he wanted to help them navigate their own journeys. Sharing his experiences—the triumphs and the setbacks—became a source of fulfillment. It reminded him of the importance of giving back and helping others find their way.

In the professional realm, James started exploring opportunities that aligned with his values and vision for a better future. He was approached by several companies and organizations impressed by his leadership and resilience. After careful consideration, he decided to join a nonprofit organization focused on developing sustainable infrastructure solutions for underserved communities. This new role allowed him to combine his expertise with his desire to make a meaningful impact.

The transition was challenging but invigorating. The nonprofit sector operated differently from the corporate world James was used to. There were fewer resources and more constraints, but the work was deeply rewarding. James thrived in this environment, finding innovative ways to solve problems and create lasting change. His leadership style evolved, becoming more collaborative and empathetic. He learned to listen more, valuing the diverse perspectives and experiences of his new colleagues.

One of the first projects James spearheaded was the development of a solar-powered water purification system for a rural village that lacked access to clean drinking water. The project brought together engineers, community leaders, and residents, all working toward a common goal. James was inspired by the passion and resilience of the community members, who were eager to learn and contribute.

As the project progressed, James found himself forming deep connections with the people he worked alongside. He listened to their stories, learned about their struggles and aspirations, and was humbled by their strength. These relationships grounded him, reminding him of the human side of his work. The project's success was not just measured in technical terms but in the tangible improvements it brought to the community's quality of life.

James's work with the nonprofit also led to speaking engagements and opportunities to share his story on a broader platform. He was invited to conferences and seminars to discuss the intersection of technology, sustainability, and community development. His talks were not just about the technical aspects of his projects but also about the personal journey that had shaped him. He spoke openly about his struggles, the betrayals, and the lessons he had learned about trust, resilience, and the importance of staying true to one's values.

These speaking engagements allowed James to connect with a wider audience, including young professionals, industry leaders, and policymakers. His message resonated with many, inspiring them to pursue their own paths with integrity and purpose. James found that sharing his story was not just cathartic but also a way to make a broader impact, encouraging others to navigate their challenges and stay committed to their values.

In his personal life, James continued to rebuild his relationships. He spent more time with his family, nurturing the bonds that had been strained by his past focus on work. He reconnected with old friends, making amends where needed and strengthening the ties that had supported him through his darkest times. These relationships became a source of joy and support, enriching his life in ways he had previously overlooked.

One day, as James stood at the top of a mountain, looking out at the vast landscape below, he felt a profound sense of peace. He had come a long way from the days of betrayal and self-doubt. The journey had been arduous, filled with highs and lows, but it had also been transformative. He realized that he had found a new sense of purpose, one that was deeply aligned with his values and passions.

James knew that the climb was far from over. There would be new challenges and obstacles, but he felt ready to face them with the strength and wisdom he had gained. He understood that true success was not just about reaching the summit but about the journey itself—the people he met, the lessons he learned, and the impact he made along the way.

As he descended the mountain, James felt a renewed sense of hope and determination. He was excited for the future, knowing that he was on a path that was true to who he was and what he believed in. The climb had taught him that every step mattered, and he was ready to continue the journey, one step at a time, with integrity, compassion, and a commitment to making a positive difference in the world.

Chapter 8: Finding Balance

James woke up to the soft glow of dawn filtering through his bedroom window. The days of feeling overwhelmed by work and personal turmoil were behind him, and he was now more focused on maintaining balance in his life. Today was a special day, one he had marked on his calendar with a mix of excitement and nostalgia.

After his morning routine, James drove to the city's community center where he had volunteered for the past year. The place was bustling with activity, children running around and adults chatting animatedly. Today was the center's annual Innovation Day, an event James had helped organize to showcase the creative projects and ideas of the young people he mentored.

James moved through the crowd, greeting familiar faces, and offering words of encouragement. He felt a deep sense of pride watching the students present their projects, each one a testament to their hard work and ingenuity. As he listened to their presentations, he was reminded of his own journey—the challenges, the triumphs, and the unwavering determination to make a difference.

One project caught his eye. A group of students had designed a prototype for a low-cost, solar-powered water filtration system, inspired by the project James had worked on in the rural village. Their enthusiasm and innovative spirit were infectious, and James could not help but feel a surge of hope for the future.

After the event, James sat with his friend and fellow mentor, Karen. They reflected on the progress the students had made and the impact their work had on the community. Karen had been a constant source of support and wisdom, and their friendship had deepened over the past year.

"You've done incredible work here, James," Karen said, her eyes shining with pride. "These kids look up to you. You have shown them what it means to overcome adversity and still stay true to your values."

James smiled, feeling a warmth spread through him. "I've learned just as much from them," he replied. "Their resilience and creativity inspire me every day. It is a reminder that no matter how tough things get, there is always a way to make a positive impact."

As the sun set, casting a golden hue over the city, James decided to take a walk. He headed towards the nearby park, a place he often visited to clear his mind and find tranquility. The park was serene, with birds chirping and leaves rustling in the gentle breeze.

James found a bench overlooking a small pond and sat down, taking in the peaceful surroundings. He thought about his journey—the highs and lows, the moments of doubt and the times of clarity. He had come a long way from the betrayal and fall that once consumed him. Now, he felt grounded, balanced, and ready for whatever lay ahead.

His phone buzzed, interrupting his thoughts. It was a message from his sister, inviting him to a family dinner next weekend. James smiled, grateful for the renewed connection with his family. He had worked hard to rebuild those relationships, understanding that they were the foundation of his support system.

As he put his phone away, a familiar voice called out his name. He looked up to see Emily, an old friend and former colleague, approaching. They had not seen each other since the turmoil at the company, and James felt a mix of surprise and joy.

"Emily, it's great to see you!" he said, standing up to give her a hug.

"James, it's been too long," Emily replied, smiling warmly. "I have heard about all the amazing work you have been doing. It is inspiring."

They sat down on the bench, catching up on each other's lives. Emily had started her own consultancy, focusing on ethical business practices and sustainability. They shared stories of their professional journeys, finding common ground in their commitment to integrity and positive change.

As they talked, James realized how much he valued these connections. His relationships had become richer and more meaningful, built on mutual respect and shared values. He felt a deep sense of gratitude for the people who had supported him and the new friendships he had formed along the way.

When they parted ways, James continued his walk, feeling a renewed sense of purpose. He thought about the future, about the projects he wanted to pursue and the lives he hoped to touch. He knew that the climb was far from over, but he felt ready to face whatever challenges lay ahead.

James returned home that evening with a full heart. He spent some time journaling, reflecting on the day and the lessons he had learned. He wrote about the importance of balance, of nurturing relationships, and of finding joy in the journey.

As he closed his journal, James felt a deep sense of peace. He understood now that success was not just about reaching the summit but about finding harmony in all aspects of life. He was grateful for the climb, with all its trials and triumphs, and looked forward to continuing the journey with integrity, compassion, and a commitment to making a positive difference in the world.

Chapter 9: Embracing Change

James stood on the stage, the bright lights casting a warm glow on the audience before him. He was at a conference for sustainable development, invited to deliver the keynote address. It was a moment he had been working towards for months, a chance to share his story and insights with a broader audience.

As he began to speak, James felt a sense of calm wash over him. He spoke about his journey, the challenges he had faced, and the lessons he had learned along the way. He emphasized the importance of resilience, integrity, and the power of community. The audience was captivated, hanging on his every word.

"For a long time, I believed that success was measured by reaching the top, by achieving goals and surpassing expectations," James said. "But I've learned that true success is about the journey, about the people we meet, the relationships we build, and the impact we make along the way."

He concluded his speech with a call to action, encouraging everyone to embrace change and to pursue their goals with passion and purpose. The applause was thunderous, and as James stepped off the stage, he felt a deep sense of fulfillment.

After the conference, James was approached by several attendees, eager to share their own stories and seek his advice. He listened with empathy, offering words of encouragement and support. These interactions reinforced his belief in the power of connection and the importance of paying it forward.

One conversation stood out. A young woman named Olivia, a recent graduate working on a renewable energy project in her hometown, shared her struggles and aspirations. James saw a lot of himself in her—driven, enthusiastic, and determined to make a difference.

"Your story is inspiring, James," Olivia said. "I am facing a lot of resistance with my project, and sometimes it feels like an uphill battle. How did you stay motivated during the toughest times?"

James smiled, recalling his own moments of doubt and uncertainty. "It's not easy," he admitted. "But what kept me going was my belief in the cause and the support of the people around me. Surround yourself with those who share your vision, and do not be afraid to lean on them when you need to. And remember, the journey itself is just as important as the destination."

Olivia thanked him, her eyes shining with renewed determination. As James watched her walk away, he felt a sense of pride and hope. He knew that the future was safe, guided by passionate and committed individuals like Olivia.

Returning home, James reflected on his own path. The nonprofit work had been incredibly rewarding, but he felt a growing desire to expand his impact even further. He started exploring new opportunities, considering how he could leverage his experiences and knowledge to drive larger-scale change.

One evening, as he sat at his kitchen table, a thought struck him. What if he combined his love for climbing with his passion for sustainable development? The idea was both exciting and daunting, but the more he thought about it, the more it made sense. He envisioned a program that used climbing as a metaphor for overcoming obstacles, fostering teamwork, and promoting environmental stewardship.

James began drafting a proposal for a new initiative, tentatively called "Climb for Change." The program would bring together young leaders from diverse backgrounds, offering them an immersive experience that combined physical challenges with leadership training and community service. Participants would not only learn about sustainability and resilience but also develop the skills and mindset needed to drive positive change in their own communities.

The response to his proposal was overwhelmingly positive. James received support from various organizations, eager to collaborate and provide resources. He assembled a dedicated team, including Karen and other trusted colleagues, to help bring the vision to life.

Over the next several months, James and his team worked tirelessly to develop the curriculum, secure funding, and plan the inaugural expedition. They reached out to schools, community centers, and youth organizations, spreading the word and encouraging applications. The excitement and enthusiasm from prospective participants were contagious, fueling James's drive to make the program a reality.

Finally, the day arrived. James stood at the base of a majestic mountain, surrounded by a group of eager young leaders. The air was crisp and filled with anticipation. As he looked at the faces around him, James felt a sense of pride and fulfillment. This was more than just a program; it was a culmination of his journey, a way to share the lessons he had learned and to inspire the next generation of changemakers.

The climb was challenging, testing their physical and mental limits. There were moments of doubt, frustration, and exhaustion. But there were also moments of triumph, teamwork, and profound connection. James watched as the participants bonded, supporting each other through the toughest parts of the climb and celebrating each milestone together.

At the summit, the group gathered for a moment of reflection. James addressed them, his voice filled with emotion. "This climb is a metaphor for life," he said. "It is not just about reaching the top but about the journey, the challenges we overcome, and the people we meet along the way. Remember this experience and carry these lessons with you. You have the power to make a difference, to lead with integrity and compassion."

As they descended, James felt a deep sense of satisfaction. Climb for Change had exceeded his expectations, proving that with the right support and mindset, young people could achieve remarkable things. He knew that this was just the beginning and that there were many more climbs and adventures ahead.

James returned home with a renewed sense of purpose. He continued to expand Climb for Change, reaching more communities and inspiring countless young leaders. His work with the nonprofit flourished, and he became a sought-after speaker and mentor, sharing his story and encouraging others to embrace change and pursue their passions.

Through it all, James remained grounded, finding balance in his personal life, and nurturing the relationships that mattered most. He had learned that success was not just about personal achievements but about the impact one had on others and the legacy one left behind.

As he stood on another mountaintop, looking out at the horizon, James felt a profound sense of gratitude. His journey had been filled with twists and turns, highs, and lows, but it had shaped him into the person he was today. He was ready to continue the climb, knowing that the journey itself was the greatest reward.

Chapter 10: Legacy of Impact

Years passed, and James found himself reflecting on the journey that had brought him to this moment. Climb for Change had grown beyond his wildest expectations, impacting communities around the world and empowering countless young leaders. What had started as a simple idea had blossomed into a global movement for sustainability, resilience, and social change.

The program had evolved, adapting to new challenges, and expanding its reach. Participants from diverse backgrounds came together to tackle environmental projects, promote community engagement, and foster leadership skills. They climbed mountains, cleaned up beaches, planted trees, and collaborated on initiatives that made a tangible difference in their communities.

James continued to lead Climb for Change with passion and dedication. He traveled extensively, visiting program sites, meeting with participants, and witnessing firsthand the transformative power of the program. Each expedition reaffirmed his belief in the potential of young people to create positive change and inspired him to push the boundaries even further.

Back home, James remained active in the nonprofit sector, advocating for sustainable development policies, and supporting initiatives that aligned with his values. He collaborated with like-minded organizations, forged partnerships with government agencies, and spoke at international conferences on environmental sustainability and youth empowerment.

Throughout it all, James remained humble, deflecting praise, and acknowledging the contributions of his team and the participants of Climb for Change. He understood that the program's success was not solely his own, but a collective effort fueled by the dedication and passion of everyone involved.

As he approached his fiftieth birthday, James decided to take stock of his life and legacy. He spent time with his family, cherishing moments with his children and grandchildren. He revisited old friendships, rekindling connections that had enriched his journey. And he reflected on the lessons he had learned—the importance of resilience, integrity, and staying true to one's values.

One evening, James received a letter from Olivia, the young woman he had met years ago at the conference. She shared news of her recent promotion to a leadership role in renewable energy advocacy, citing Climb for Change as a pivotal influence in her career. The letter filled James with pride and reinforced his belief in the ripple effect of positive actions.

As he read Olivia's words, James thought about the impact he had made—not just through Climb for Change but through his commitment to integrity, compassion, and making a difference in the world. His journey had been filled with challenges and triumphs, setbacks, and successes, but through it all, he had remained steadfast in his pursuit of a better future for generations to come.

Looking out at the sunset from his home office, James felt a deep sense of contentment. He knew that his legacy would live on through the lives he had touched and the changes he had inspired. Climb for Change had become more than a program—it was a testament to the power of resilience, community, and the belief that each person can create positive change.

As James closed his eyes that night, he felt a profound gratitude for the journey that had shaped him into the person he had become. The climb had been challenging, but it had also been filled with moments of joy, growth, and profound connection. He knew that the best was yet to come, and he was excited to continue his journey, leaving a legacy of impact and inspiration.

Chapter 11: Reflections and New Horizons

James sat at his desk, surrounded by the mementos and memories of a lifetime of adventures and accomplishments. The sun streamed through the window, casting a warm glow on the photos and souvenirs that lined the shelves. He took a sip of his coffee and gazed out at the serene landscape beyond his home.

It had been several years since he had retired from active leadership in Climb for Change. The program continued to thrive under new leadership, expanding its reach and impact with each passing year. James remained involved as a mentor and advisor, offering guidance to the next generation of leaders who carried forward the mission he had started.

Retirement had brought a slower pace of life, allowing James to indulge in his love for writing and photography. He had always been drawn to capturing moments—both big and small—that told stories of resilience, hope, and the beauty of the natural world. His photographs had been featured in exhibitions and publications, each image a reflection of his deep connection to the places he had visited and the people he had met along the way.

One of his proudest moments had been publishing his memoir, titled "From the Valley to the Summit: A Journey of Resilience and Impact." The book chronicled his life's journey—from the challenges of his early years to the triumphs and setbacks he had faced as a leader and advocate for sustainable development. It was a testament to the power of perseverance and the belief that every obstacle could be overcome with courage and determination.

The response to the memoir had been overwhelmingly positive. Readers from around the world reached out to share their own stories of resilience and inspiration, connecting deeply with James's message of hope and resilience. He received letters and emails expressing gratitude for sharing his journey so openly and for providing a roadmap for navigating life's challenges with grace and integrity.

As he reflected on his life's work, James felt a deep sense of fulfillment. He had dedicated his career to making a difference, whether through Climb for

Change, his advocacy work, or his writings. He had learned valuable lessons along the way—about leadership, collaboration, and the importance of staying true to one's values—and he hoped to pass on those lessons to future generations.

One sunny afternoon, James received an unexpected invitation to speak at a prestigious university. The topic was leadership in times of uncertainty, a subject close to his heart. He accepted the invitation eagerly, seeing it as an opportunity to inspire and empower young minds to embrace change and lead with compassion and integrity.

Standing before the eager audience, James felt a familiar rush of adrenaline. He spoke from the heart, drawing on his experiences and the lessons he had learned throughout his career. He encouraged the students to take risks, to challenge the status quo, and to never lose sight of their values in the pursuit of success.

After the talk, several students approached James, eager to ask questions and seek advice. He listened attentively, offering words of wisdom and encouragement. He saw his younger self reflected in their earnest expressions and felt a deep sense of hope for the future.

As he drove home that evening, James thought about the journey that had led him to this moment. He had climbed many mountains—both literal and figurative—and had emerged stronger and more resilient with each ascent. Retirement had not marked the end of his journey, but the beginning of a new chapter filled with opportunities to share his experiences and wisdom.

In the quiet of his study, James picked up a pen and began jotting down ideas for his next book. He wanted to delve deeper into the principles of leadership, resilience, and sustainable development, exploring how individuals and organizations could drive meaningful change in a rapidly changing world. It was a new challenge, a new mountain to climb, and James embraced it with the same passion and determination that had guided him throughout his life.

As he wrote, James felt a profound sense of gratitude for the opportunities he had been given, the people he had met, and the impact he had made. He knew that the journey was far from over, and he looked forward to the adventures and discoveries that lay ahead.

The sun set on another day, casting a golden hue over the landscape. James closed his notebook with a smile, knowing that he had found his purpose in helping others find theirs. With a heart full of gratitude and a mind full of dreams, he embraced the future, ready to continue his journey of resilience, impact, and lifelong learning.

And so, the story of James's life continued—a testament to the power of courage, compassion, and the belief that each person can make a difference in the world.

Dear Readers,

As you close the last chapter of James's journey, I invite you to reflect on the profound lessons of resilience, integrity, and impact that have unfolded. James's story is not just one of personal triumph but a testament to the transformative power of perseverance and compassion.

Now, I call upon each of you to consider how you can contribute to positive change in your own lives and communities. Whether it is through small acts of kindness, volunteering your time for a cause you believe in, or advocating for policies that promote sustainability and social justice, your actions matter.

Embrace challenges as opportunities for growth. Stand up for what you believe in, even when it is difficult. And remember, the journey to creating a better world begins with each of us, taking steps—big or small—towards a common goal of a more inclusive, sustainable, and compassionate society.

Let James's story inspire you to lead with courage, to foster meaningful connections, and to leave a legacy of impact. Together, we can build a future where every individual can thrive, where resilience and empathy guide our decisions, and where each act of kindness ripples outward, creating waves of positive change.

Thank you for joining us on this journey. Your commitment to making a difference makes all the difference.

With hope and determination,

DeShaun "HeartFlare" Williams

Afterword

As I conclude the journey chronicled in these pages, I am reminded of the profound impact that each of us can have on the world around us. This book has been a testament to resilience, integrity, and the power of community—themes that resonate deeply in our shared human experience.

Throughout my life, I have been privileged to witness firsthand the transformative effects of perseverance and compassion. From the valleys of hardship to the summits of achievement, I have learned that every setback is an opportunity for growth, every challenge a chance to reaffirm our commitment to making a difference.

I hope that my story has inspired you to embrace your own journey of resilience and impact. Whether you find yourself facing personal struggles or navigating global issues, know that your actions matter. Small gestures of kindness, acts of courage, and steadfast commitment to your values can create ripple effects far beyond what you imagine.

Remember, the journey towards a better world is not a solitary path. It is woven together by the collective efforts of individuals like you—individuals who dare to dream, who strive for justice, and who believe in the possibility of a brighter future.

As you close this book, I encourage you to reflect on the lessons learned, the challenges overcome, and the moments of joy and connection that have shaped your own journey. Let us continue to build bridges, to lift each other up, and to leave a legacy of compassion and resilience for generations to come.

Thank you for sharing this journey with me. May we all find strength in our stories, courage in our convictions, and hope in our hearts as we navigate the paths ahead.

With gratitude and warmest regards,

DeShaun "HeartFlare" Williams

Made in the USA
Columbia, SC
04 October 2024